A RAFT OF SEA OTTERS

An *affectionate portrait*

TEXT
Vicki León

PHOTOGRAPHS
Richard Bucich & Jeff Foott

ADDITIONAL PHOTOGRAPHS
Charles Bancroft, Batista-Moon Studio,
Charles Deutsch, John Gerlach, François Gohier,
Richard Hansen, Stephen Krasemann, George Lepp,
Tom Mangelsen, Steve Rosenberg & Doug Wechsler

BOOK & MAP DESIGN
Ashala Nicols-Lawler

ILLUSTRATIONS
Cathi Von Schimmelmann

© 1987, revised 1988 Blake Publishing
a division of the Graphic Center
2222 Beebee Street, San Luis Obispo California 93401
Printed in the United States of America.
ISBN 0-918303-13-3

A long 220 miles of California's coastline live the southern sea otters, less than 1,700 of them, the resilient remnants of a population that once numbered close to 18,000. These appealing marine mammals with the teddybear faces spend their lives among the icy waves. You will often see them in little groups, bobbing like corks among the fronds of the giant kelp plants that sway just offshore.

Like "flock" or "herd," the word "raft" describes a group of sea otters. At a distance, the wet brown bodies of the otters do resemble a loosely organized raft of logs. But the word "raft" can mean more. It perfectly conveys the Huck Finn quality   of sea otter life: limitless, free, full of risk and exhilaration in equal measure. "Raft" also echoes the tenacity of this little animal, who has returned from the brink of extinction in the 19th century, only to be faced by new threats to its survival in the 20th.

For a few million years, this species called *Enhydra lutris* frolicked along the Pacific coast,

ranging from Baja California north to Alaska and along the Aleutian Islands to the remote Kuril Islands of Japan. For at least 7,500 of those years, sea otters coexisted peacefully with the Native American population. Otters and humans shared the shoreline resources of abalone, clam, urchin and crab.

Two hundred years ago, fur hunters from Europe, Russia and America began to kill sea otters. Because the otters were so trusting, it was child's play. Over a 140-year span, hunters killed nearly half a million otters, goaded by the immense profits the soft furs offered. At first, pelts brought $10 each, then $60. By 1900, when the animal was clearly on the wane, the price per pelt rose to $1,125. Soon there were no animals to be found at any price.

The sea otter, meanwhile, was lying low. Several pathetically small groups remained alive, overlooked by hunters. In the curious way that humans have of making amends, international legislation protecting the sea otter had been enacted in 1911, even though it was thought there were few if any animals left to protect.

The world learned of California's survivors in 1938. That year, coastal Highway One through Big Sur was officially opened to road traffic. Bixby Creek, over which the highway passed, had been the hiding place for a raft of sea otters.

Otters dive for food and to find rock tools to get into their dinners. Dives commonly take one to two minutes. Prickly as they look, giant purple sea urchins are a favorite menu item. Some otters eat so many urchins in their lifetime that their teeth and bones turn a beautiful shade of lavender.

The southern sea otter began its slow comeback. By 1986, it occupied about 10% of its original range. In California, you can now spot otters from Año Nuevo in San Mateo County south to the Santa Maria River, the boundary between San Luis Obispo and Santa Barbara Counties.

Its cousin, the northern sea otter, suffered similar losses from hunters. Being a larger, more isolated population, however, the northern otter recovered more fully in Alaskan waters. Small groups have been reestablished in British Columbia and Washington also.

Mother Nature saw fit to make the Pacific Ocean the icy home for this warm-blooded cousin

Because sea otters need to groom so much, you'd think it would be easier for them to groom on dry land. And on rare occasions, an otter will do just that. But sea otters feel safest and happiest at sea.

of the mink. Unlike seals and whales, the sea otter is not equipped with a layer of blubber to keep warm. Instead, the otter has the most luxuriant coat of fur in the world. When you first see an otter grooming himself, your first thought is: His fur is a size too big. Or maybe a couple of sizes too big. But the otter is built that way for a special reason.

It isn't just fur that keeps the sea otter warm in the water. It is the air which the otter traps among its 800 million hairs that provides insulation. And the way the otter gets air next to its skin is through grooming – lots of it. The sea otter spends at least 10% of its life cleaning its fur, squeezing or licking

water out of it, and blowing or rolling air into it. With all this grooming to do on every part of the body, you can see the benefits of having a very loose coat of fur. It lets you get to all the hard-to-reach places.

Despite being sociable animals, sea otters don't groom each other the way that primates and other animals do. The only exceptions are mothers and pups. For the first few months of a pup's life, its mother is so busy grooming, warming and feeding the pup that she scarcely has time to keep her own fur decent.

The sea otter's other strategy for survival in the sea is a high metabolic rate. Its body temperature is 100 degrees Fahrenheit, which has to be fueled by large amounts of calories. The sea otter spends about 25% of its time foraging for food. It needs to consume nearly one-quarter of its body weight each day in order to live.

Attention has often focused on the few items that otters and humans compete for. But many things that otters eat are not found on human dinner tables. Otters choose from a smorgasbord. They eat foods such as sea urchins, ten types of clams, worms, chitons, abalone, octopus, barnacles, sea cucumbers, seasonal foods like squid and the occasional chewy starfish. Interestingly, otters are like humans in their strong individual preferences. One otter may eat nothing but kelp crab and urchins. Another may be a turban snail and squid fancier. Recent research has also revealed that female sea otters sometimes change their diet preferences once they have young.

It is hard work foraging, as any otter will tell

you. Otters forage about three times each 24 hours, usually leaving their rafting and resting area to do so. Most of their food is on the bottom and they typically dive 15 to 50 feet to find it.

A sea otter must use his whiskers, front paws, nose and eyes to locate the prey. Then he has to catch it or dislodge it. If it is a mollusk, the sea otter first looks around for a rock on the ocean floor to help him. It sometimes takes repeated dives and dozens of whacks with a rock to break loose a difficult-to-move mollusk like the abalone. What with prey to find, rocks to collect and pounding to do, dives can last as long as four minutes.

Underwater, the sea otter swims rapidly through the kelp forest. Using his broad tail and big feet, the otter flaps his hindquarters in an oddly comic yet effective swimming style. Speed and agility are important to the sea otter. For many of his groceries, the sea otter has competitors – seals, wolf eels, fishes, and humans.

One of the sea otter's adaptations is his "purse:" an extra fold of skin under his armpits, handy for stashing food and rocks for a return to the surface.

Once at the surface, the sea otter rolls onto his back and spreads his catch out onto the picnic table of his belly. Some otters like to use a rock as an anvil to break shells against. Others bang shell against shell, or use a smaller stone to whack away at the food. In any case, otter dining is characterized by a series of impatient little tap-tap-taps. (That distinctive sound made it even easier for the fur hunters of the last century to locate their victims.)

Sea otters are one of the few tool-using animals in the world. They select rocks for use as underwater sledgehammers and on the surface as anvils and picks.

Even while dining on messy crab or sea urchins, sea otters like to keep scrupulously neat. They periodically roll in the water, washing their chests of scraps, all the while keeping head and paws dry. Dining otters are popular with seagulls and small fish, who often hang around to catch the free tidbits.

"*Years ago in France, I read of Jacques Cousteau's work with sea otters and I dreamt of working with them too. Now, each time I photograph sea otters, I feel a new sense of wonder at this resilient little animal.*"
— François Gohier, nature photographer

When full-grown, the sea otter is about the size of a German shepherd. Males weigh about 60 pounds; females, 30% less. In their ocean environment, they appear much smaller. Bobbing among the giant swells of the Pacific, their round heads look as tiny and gallant as the ships of Christopher Columbus must have appeared.

Sea otters are California's wildlife show. Unlike the shyer citizens of the ocean, sea otters' lives are on public display, daily, along 220 miles of our coast.

"The sea otter is perhaps the only wild creature whose entire life cycle – birth, eating, playing, grooming, mating, raising young – can easily be observed by man without harm to the animal. It is an incredible opportunity. And a weighty responsibility. For we have to see that the habitat in which these beautiful and trusting animals live is not destroyed or contaminated," says Carol Fulton, Executive Director of Friends of the Sea Otter, a 5,000-member international organization dedicated

to the preservation of the California sea otter and its habitat.

The otters' habitat is that portion of the ocean which lies up to 1 1/2 miles offshore. It is bordered by the great kelp beds. On the surface, the glistening bulbs and long caramel-colored fronds of the giant kelp form a loose net in the water, one which cuts wave action and provides security and convenient anchor holds for the sea otter. Dive below the surface, and you see the kelp as it truly is – a glorious dancing forest of trees up to 100 feet tall –" the sequoias of the sea," as Jacques Cousteau calls them.

Otters groom alone and in groups called rafts. They can spend up to three hours a day at it. Sometimes you'll see bright tags on their flippers. Tagging identifies individuals, helps track birth and mortality rates and defines otter home territories for biologists.

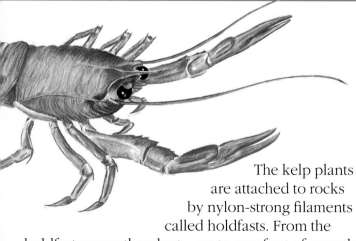

The kelp plants are attached to rocks by nylon-strong filaments called holdfasts. From the holdfast grows the plant – up to one foot of growth per day. Kelp fronds, like the leaves of a deciduous tree, die and fall off after six months of furious activity. Sustained by the balloon-like bulbs on their leaves, the kelp trees sway rhythmically toward the surface, the ceiling of their world.

Besides otters, a huge number of living creatures call the kelp forest home. Over 30 species of fish, 80 species of algae, and more than 300 kinds of macroinvertebrates – from starfish to abalone – live and grow here.

A kelp forest is one of the most productive habitats on earth. It supports 300 pounds of fish per acre – three times as much fish as can live in ocean terrain without kelp.

Sea otters do most of their food gathering in the kelp forest. They perform an important service

*A **wonderfully flexible** animal, the sea otter can roll in the water without even getting his head or paws wet. Rolling and somersaulting are two ways in which otters get air into their fur. Air provides insulation vital for their survival in the icy Pacific Ocean.*

by consuming large quantities of sea urchins. The urchin, a prickly fellow, has a huge appetite for kelp. Urchins in excess are a serious threat to the kelp forest. The sea otter is just one factor that helps balance the tightly interdependent marine community of the kelp forest.

Over the millions of years he has been around, the sea otter has developed some interesting adaptations for his marine life. One is his peculiar-looking hind foot: long and flipper-like, it has a very long outside toe which lets the otter swim more efficiently on his back.

Another adaptation of the otter is its extreme flexibility. In the water, an otter can go from lying

on his back to sitting up just as easily as you can on land. In order to catch prey and open it, the sea otter has also developed front paws which are both strong and nimble.

A strong swimmer, the otter swims mainly on his back but can roll onto his stomach without missing a stroke or even getting his paws wet. Underwater, sea otters can attain 2.2 miles per hour – pretty impressive for an animal whose gangly, every-which-way swimming style resembles a clown wearing big shoes.

The characteristic resting position of otters is on their backs in the water, head well up, paws and flippers stiffly extended. It looks as though they have just painted their nails, and are waiting for the polish to dry. But the purpose of keeping their paws and flippers out of the water is heat regulation. They are about the only place on a sea otter's body without heavy fur insulation. Keeping them dry saves energy and calories.

On his great marine waterbed, an otter sleeps with utmost tranquility, paws often folded on his chest. Otters spend more than half their time sleeping or resting. This also helps conserve calories which are expended so heavily during food-seeking bouts that occupy up to eight hours

per day. After eating, the otter invariably grooms himself and then naps or sleeps.

The exception of course is the mother otter. When her pup is young, she gets about as much rest as the average human mother – that is to say, almost none. The pup practically lives on her chest for several months. Even while the pup is sleeping, the mother grooms and warms it. From birth, the pup nurses on mother's milk. Soon it is introduced to solid food. The mother swims slowly on her back, twisting her head so that one eye can scan underwater for prey. Once she has found a good

spot, she carefully floats the pup and dives. When she comes up with dinner, she shells it and offers bites to the pup, who before long is eating with gusto. By 14 weeks, most pups have learned to swim, dive and groom themselves. While their mother dives for food, they can now peer anxiously into the water, keeping an eye on her.

Even from infancy, the sea otter's diet is crunchy: solid foods such as crab, snails and clams are quickly given to the pup in addition to the mother's fat-rich milk. To help them grapple with their diet, sea otter pups are born with a full set of

Female otters often live and move about within one special area. Males are even more mobile, usually roaming within a huge home territory.

32 teeth. This combination of broad flat molars and rounded blunt canines gives them the potential to eat the full range of adult sea otter menu items. Researchers have discovered that sea otter pups have food likes and dislikes. They often prefer their food "pre-shelled," rejecting items until the mother otter patiently prepares them. Although they do not use tools for themselves yet, pups soon learn to imitate how food-opening is accomplished. You can sometimes see slightly older pups pounding their little chests in what looks like dress rehearsal for rock tool use.

"*The welfare of the animal remains the most important thing for me. My relationship with wildlife is one of mutual respect.*"
— Jeff Foott, wilderness photographer

California sea otters
*spend almost every moment
of their lives in the water.
Very occasionally, however,
they come ashore for a
brief time, to rest upon
algae-covered rocks or upon
the beach. This activity is
called "hauling out."*

*Once, long ago,
California otters probably
spent more time on land,
the way their Alaskan
cousins still do. Perhaps the
memory of their terrible
vulnerability to the hunters
of last century still lingers.*

*Today, concerned
humans who are lucky
enough to witness a rare
land visit tend to protect
the otters by keeping the
details of time and place
a secret.*

The sea otter has a playful and curious nature, one which apparently allows it to raft trustingly close to human activity. The floating communities called rafts contain as few as two otters and as many as 20. Otters raft together primarily for resting and socializing, leaving the raft area to forage for food.

Sociable and non-aggressive as they are, sea otters nevertheless lead sexually segregated lives.

Most females raft with other females, with or without pups. Males generally raft together, sometimes quite a distance from the females. Occasionally a solitary male will maintain his own territory within a female-dominated area.

As with any animal, the sea otter young are the most playful. Adult otters of both sexes often allow pups to climb over them. Older pups will often tumble younger otters, boisterously using them as toys until their mothers snap at them.

Otter-watching is fascinating fun. Not only are the animals lively, but they are often highly individual in appearance. The hardest part is

guessing sex and age. Otters with pink or scarred noses are likely to be females. White or grizzled fur around the head usually indicates an older otter. Up to three months of age, pups are readily noticeable because of their fluffy baby fur, the color of taffy.

Sea otters do not have permanent mates. Rather, they join together for brief interludes, which may occur any time of year. The male approaches the female. At first, all is calm and tenderness. The otters cuddle, murmur and touch, softly braiding their bodies together as they roll, over and over, on the water's surface. Gradually they become wilder, fiercer. At this point, the male loses his gentle

"Sea otters are a lot like people.
The ones that are the most trusting
end up risking the most."
— Richard Bucich, wildlife photographer

A tireless teacher, the *mother otter demonstrates tenderness and affection to her pup as well as the rudiments of swimming, grooming and diving for food. Not all behaviors have to be learned. Pups are born knowing how to nurse and to keep their paws dry.*

nature and attaches himself to the female by biting her nose. From a human standpoint, it looks cruel. But getting a grip on something solid in this movable and slippery ocean environment is probably a biological necessity for the male sea otter.

For three to five days, the otters stay together, eating, resting and mating. In the end, it is the female who leaves the male. Bloody nosed, she rejoins her raft and he returns to his own favored territory.

The sea otter mother is a single parent. Except for mating, the two adult sexes don't interact much, and sea otter fathers don't play much part in raising pups. That task is up to the female, who deserves a "Mother of the Year" award for her devotion.

Pup care is almost non-stop for the first few months of life. The baby lives on the mother's chest, and the two of them often raft alone. So where does the mother park the baby when she needs to dive for groceries? The answer is ingenious. Pups are born with an important safety device: buoyancy. They cannot swim yet, but they cannot drown either. So mother otter leaves the pup, sometimes anchoring it to a strand of kelp, dives and returns with food.

She is unerringly guided back to the pup by its other safety feature: a piping cry, which it emits as steadily as a lighthouse foghorn when mother is not in sight. At birth, a pup weighs between three and

five pounds and resembles a ball of dandelion fluff with two bright eyes. It is astonishing to hear the amount of noise that one small ball of fluff can generate. The sound carries over the roar of the waves, the squawks of the gulls, and probably over the whine of a buzzsaw if need be.

Pups are born mimics and a good thing too: they have much to learn during the six months or so in which they are dependent. Eating solid food and swimming are the pup's first accomplishments. Diving, grooming, catching prey and tool-using come later.

When pups are older, they are easy to spot.

They often nurse, float or cuddle at right angles to their mothers. You may also see them boldly stealing food from their mothers, an activity that later evolves into calm sharing.

With the day-and-night care involved in pup-raising, it is no wonder that sea otters usually give birth to just one pup at a time. Despite maternal devotion, mortality among pups can be disturbingly high some years. The greatest danger they face are harsh winter storms, which sometimes separate pups from their mothers to die of exposure on the shore or at sea.

> **Because capture is** traumatic for any wild creature, otter monitoring is a painstaking operation. Agencies such as the California Department of Fish and Game carefully catch otters with a hand-held underwater trap, then weigh and examine them.

Luckily for sea otters, they do have some friends on shore. Over the years, a number of otter pups orphaned on California beaches have been rescued by caring humans. Some have been raised until they can care for themselves and then returned to the wild. Others now lead pampered lives in aquariums along the Pacific coast.

Human curiosity and caring about the otter extends in other directions. Because the southern sea otter is designated as a threatened species, it is the subject of much scientific study. Agencies such as the U.S. Fish and Wildlife Service and the California Department of Fish and Game monitor the otters through field observations and tagging programs. Tagging is used to track the movement and activities of populations and individuals. Over 400 otters have now been tagged.

Part of human concern focuses on the small size of the southern sea otter population. Although the otters continue to extend their range geographically, their numbers have remained almost level over the last decade.

Sea otters face a number of threats to their

Before release, some sea otters are tagged with home territory and/or individual identification tags. These readily visible tags, clipped to otter flippers, help researchers learn important data about the fragile California sea otter population.

survival, almost all of them connected with human activity. Nets set for fish have accidentally killed a large number of otters. Deliberate shootings have further diminished the population. But the greatest threat is that of contamination: an oil tanker spill or leaks from offshore drilling.

Oil contamination can quickly kill otters. If as little as one-quarter of an otter's fur becomes soiled, the otter cannot groom his coat for warmth. He will almost surely freeze to death. Oil is toxic when eaten by otters. If the animal eats a quantity of oil on his food or while trying to groom himself, he could also die. In the event of an oil spill, experts

consider the capture, cleanup and rescue of otters to be an almost hopeless task.

Supporters of this vulnerable animal advocate what they call a sea otter insurance policy. This plan, still in its preliminary stages, calls for the establishment of a reserve breeding colony of sea otters on San Nicolas Island. Up to 250 otters have begun to be translocated to San Nicolas, the remotest of the Channel Islands. In case an oil spill occurs off the coast of California, it is hoped that the otter population at San Nicolas would escape contamination.

Biologists call the sea otter a "foundation

species." This means that otters play a major role in the health of the nearshore habitat, especially the kelp forest. Studies among Alaskan otters show that a population of 60 otters per square mile is associated with dense kelp beds and a rich community of fish and other marine life. A population of zero otters, on the other hand, is associated with huge numbers of sea urchins, little or no kelp and a greatly reduced diversity of marine life.

These findings are hotly contested by local shellfishermen, whose opinion is that otters wipe out shellfish resources wherever they go. It is certainly true that otters eat quantities of abalone and other shellfish. And it is true that they are unhampered by human restrictions about size, number and season. But it is hard to imagine what 1,700 sea otters could do to the abalone and Pismo clam populations that hasn't already been done to them by 27 million Californians. A brief look at the over-exploitation and massive waste of our shellfish resources over the last century will confirm that.

Let's look at sea otters for what they are: marine creatures with a key part to play in the balance of California's nearshore habitat. They are restorers of natural balance, not its ravagers. That

role, unfortunately, is a human specialty. Sea otters are a symbol of an incredible resource that California is still blessed with: the Pacific Ocean. By keeping it uncontaminated for otters, we also keep the ocean safe and productive for humans.

Sea otters play another role in our hearts. They are willing to let us observe them. And in doing so, the simple joy with which they live their lives enriches us, the watchers.

***Orphaned or stranded** otters have often found good homes in West Coast aquariums. One of the best sea otter rehabilitation programs is carried out by the Monterey Bay Aquarium staff, pictured right. Pups such as this one frequently grace the sea otter exhibit at the Aquarium.*

SPECIAL THANKS & ACKNOWLEGMENTS

The 38 photos selected to appear in this book represent the most memorable sea otter photographs to appear anywhere. They were taken by 13 consummately talented photographers, whose work it is our special privilege to present. Our special thanks also to William E. Townsend, Jr., of the Monterey Bay Aquarium, who acted as photographic liaison for the book; Marianne Riedman, head of the sea otter research project at the Monterey Bay Aquarium; and the sea otter researchers and biologists with the University of California, Santa Cruz.

Principal photographers

Richard Bucich: front cover; page 7; page 17; pages 22-23; page 24; page 25 upper right (courtesy of Earthviews); pages 26-27; page 30; page 31 lower right.

Jeff Foott: pages 2-3; pages 4-5; page 8; page 14-15 (courtesy of Bruce Coleman); page 18; centerfold pages 20-21; page 32; page 34; pages 38-39; page 40; inside back cover.

◆ *For further information* on how you can help protect the California sea otter, please contact Friends of the Sea Otter, P.O. Box 221220, Carmel, California 93922. Or visit their Sea Otter Center, open Monday through Saturday from 10 a.m. to 3 p.m., Sundays noon to 3 p.m., at The Crossroads Shopping Center, Rio Road and Highway One in Carmel. Phone: (408) 625-3290.

◆ *Additional information* and exhibits on sea otters can be found at aquaria all along the Pacific coast, including the Monterey Bay Aquarium, Seattle Aquarium, and the Vancouver B.C. Aquarium, and at marine life parks such as Sea World and Marine World.

◆ *Recommended reading*: *The Otter Raft*, a newsletter published by Friends of the Sea Otter, address above. For detailed information, read *The California Sea Otter: Saved or Doomed?* by John Woolfenden.

"Is man a keeper or an ally? To guard the sea otter, we cannot direct him nor can we protect him from his environment. But as his ally, we can guard the quality of our shared environment – the coastal waters. Yes, we are allies, the sea otters and ourselves – together we share a world with narrowing boundaries."

— Margaret Owings, conservationist and Founding President of Friends of the Sea Otter